I0791224

The Essential Schizophrenia Companion

ROBERT FRANCIS

with Foreword by Elyn R. Saks, author of
*The Center Cannot Hold: My Journey
through Madness*

THE ESSENTIAL SCHIZOPHRENIA COMPANION

iUniverse books may be ordered through booksellers or by contacting:

iUniverse
1663 Liberty Drive
Bloomington, IN 47403
www.iuniverse.com
844-349-9409

Because of the dynamic nature of the Internet, any web addresses or links contained in this book may have changed since publication and may no longer be valid. The views expressed in this work are solely those of the author and do not necessarily reflect the views of the publisher, and the publisher hereby disclaims any responsibility for them.

Any people depicted in stock imagery provided by Getty Images are models, and such images are being used for illustrative purposes only.
Certain stock imagery © Getty Images.

ISBN: 978-1-6632-0860-6 (sc)
ISBN: 978-1-6632-0861-3 (e)

Library of Congress Control Number: 2020917157

Print information available on the last page.

iUniverse rev. date: 09/23/2020

If you are walking on a path thick with brambles and rocks, a path that abruptly twists and turns, it's easy to get lost, or tired, or discouraged. You might be tempted to give up entirely. But if a kind and patient person comes along and takes your hand, saying, "I see you're having a hard time- here, follow me, I'll help you find your way," the path becomes manageable, the journey less frightening.

— Elyn R. Saks, *The Center Cannot Hold: My Journey through Madness*

CONTENTS

FOREWORD

Elyn R. Saks

Robert Francis's book *The Essential Schizophrenia Companion* is a smart and moving account of living with schizophrenia. Robert is a therapist himself who lives with schizophrenia, and telling his story should be of great use to people who suffer with schizophrenia, their families, and their close friends—and indeed, to members of the general public.

First, Robert takes the reader through the basics of his history—who he is. He next discusses the concept of schizophrenia, issues such as its distinction from mood disorders and the nature of its symptoms (e.g., delusions and hallucinations). He notes also that the presentation of schizophrenia can be very different in different people.

His discussion of anosognosia is thoughtful and well taken. He believes that helping patients see that they lack insight is very important to get them on the same page about treatment. (On the other hand, you can get people interested in treatment even if they lack insight by appealing to things they are experiencing and don't like, such as sleeplessness.)

Robert next has an interesting discussion of the paradoxical nature of schizophrenia and how, once the patient becomes comfortable with "routine cognitive paradox, miracles happen, and yet twice again!"

By *behavioral rationality*, Robert means that in the midst of difficult and scary symptoms, he is able to "practice a sort of manneristic reasonableness." A colleague of mine, with bipolar disorder, and I talk about this as "passing as normal." It allows one to live in one's work and personal worlds without facing the stigma one would confront if public about one's illness.

In the chapter "Protective Factors," Robert discusses as one of his primary ones his taking antipsychotic medicine for over twenty-five years. He recognizes there are disputes in society about taking these and believes people should make their own best judgments. The medicine he has been on is called clozapine. (It is the Cadillac of efficacy but is cumbersome, requiring lots of blood tests, so it is only used if a patient fails on other drugs.)

Robert also makes good use of psychotherapy. It used to be thought that meds alone were sufficient for treating schizophrenia, but it is now recognized that the treatment of choice is medication combined with some form of psychosocial treatment.

One way Robert makes use of therapy is when his therapist does some "reality testing" for him, pointing out that his perceptions are significantly distorted. This actually brings him back to reality.

Robert's lifestyle generally is healthy: he doesn't drink or do drugs, exercises regularly, sleeps well, and he fills his life with enjoyable things such as fantasy football. He also gets great benefit from his faith in God.

Robert speaks interestingly about philosophy of mind and its connection with schizophrenia. For example, he "wonders if [his] mind is indeed differentiated from the rest." Many people with schizophrenia, he says, have delusions that "reflect a reality that challenges the very presumption of differentiated minds."

Robert lays out thoughts about different kinds and genres of research, including studies of medication treatment and psychosocial interventions.

He ends with a chapter titled "Putting It All Together," noting, for example, that we all have challenges of one kind or another. He also points out how humor has been helpful in his life: "It's okay to laugh at psychosis."

In all, *The Essential Schizophrenia Companion* is a profound, moving, and thoughtful account of living life with a serious mental illness. It is said that putting a human face on mental illness is the best way to reduce stigma. *The Essential Schizophrenia Companion* meets this calling and does so in spades!

Enjoy your read!

INTRODUCTION

As we depart on our literary journey, my dear reader, let me first supply the vessel for our travel. We will need a few bits of knowledge prior to departure. First, *The Essential Schizophrenia Companion* is a follow-up volume to my first book on schizophrenia entitled *On Conquering Schizophrenia: From the Desk of a Therapist and Survivor, with Purview on Metaphysics, Philosophy, and Theology.* In this newest literary venture, there will be certain similarities and differences to the one prior. Allow me to explain.

As far as the similarities, we must of course start with authorship: it is I who wrote it. Further similarity will involve the target of the relegation of schizophrenia. In purpose, this is similar to the last. A final similarity will be in my writing style. More specifically yet, my writing style pushes my voice to you. I'm writing directly to you, reader, and I do so with the utmost respect for your own brilliance and shining soul. I never patronize, because I know of your own personal brilliance. As such, I am honored by your readership. So it is together that we launch on our literary journey. I truly appreciate your company and find you a soothing presence. Your brilliance illuminates my literation! I thank you for your accompaniment.

If you read my previous book, you know that I dabbled in various genres, including metaphysics, philosophy, and theology. My target was the relegation and mitigation of schizophrenia, and these genres were my tools to do so. This volume will resonate similarly in that the priority is the defeat of the wily foe known as schizophrenia. This is unchanged from the last. However, this volume lacks the genre meandering of the last. This book is more pointed. Each chapter resides of its own accord and can be read singularly or randomly, as well as by its customary ordination.

And so, my dear reader, we begin a new journey of friendship joined by the common theme of the defeat of the ever elusive and enigmatic parlance known as schizophrenia. Along the way, let us not forget our capacity for a shared humor. If one cannot laugh at one's troubles, they will double! Our topic is a serious one, but let us not be thrust into an unnecessary melancholia. Schizophrenia is a formidable foe but also subject to some comedic relief. Please, I urge you to never forget the everlasting salve and palliation of a good humor!

Beyond any veneer, and because of my deep affinity for each and every reader, I again heartily adopt my salutatory phrasing that originated in *On Conquering Schizophrenia*: "my dear reader." This is a term of great endearment. I am privileged by your readership, and I thank you.

As a literary note, I have included a short glossary at the end of *The Essential Schizophrenia Companion* for easy reference. It includes the definitions to all the pertinent schizophrenia symptoms. In relation to you and yours, please refer as may be needed.

Last, it is important to know that I write creatively. I do not draw from the writings of others, so there are no citations. In this manner, I am most proficient. Let it be known, loud and clear, that this is not a volume of science. Rather, it is one of the humanities. Please keep this in mind! Let us now together proceed, my dear reader, on our path laid forward, otherwise known as *The Essential Schizophrenia Companion*.

CHAPTER 1

WHO AM I?

Before we launch into the elements of *The Essential Schizophrenia Companion*, please allow me, my dear reader, to provide some nuance as to who I am in relation to my authorship. My name is Robert Francis. I previously wrote a book entitled *On Conquering Schizophrenia: From the Desk of a Therapist and Survivor*. *The Essential Schizophrenia Companion* is my second venture of writing on the topic of schizophrenia. So you can best immerse yourself in this proper literary context, I offer some more facts as to my life characteristics and qualities.

I was diagnosed with schizophrenia when I was about twenty-four years old. I have lived with it to this day. I am now a hearty forty-nine years old. If my mathematics is proper, the remains are a quarter century living with schizophrenia and its entanglement. Although I have learned quite capably, I think, to function despite the schizophrenia, my symptoms do not yield. Schizophrenia is a progressive-type disease, meaning it persists over time and offers no cure. However, with the absence of a cure comes gainful reconciliation. *The Essential Schizophrenia Companion* is a book about living life with schizophrenia similarly to the rest of our shared humanity. It is about gainfully living a full life in all one's chosen life realms. Schizophrenia may be a bump in the road or a thorn in one's side (whichever metaphor best suits), but each and every human being ever to traverse this beautiful Earth has had his or her own personal challenges. Therefore, I see schizophrenia as a personal challenge much akin to the struggles of my neighbor, only differentiated by its challenging type or its category.

I am a licensed clinical social worker (LCSW). I have a bachelor of arts and a master's in social work. I have been working as a talk therapist now for some fifteen years. My domain is mental health, and I have worked in a variety of mental health settings. In my professional realm, I never have told those I work with that I have schizophrenia. By manner of a personal choice, I have always preferred to keep schizophrenia as a private medical condition. Further, the only people who know of my schizophrenia are my family members. I choose not to tell even friends or acquaintances.

I want you to know that Robert Francis is a pen name. I write under a pen name for my own sense of confidentiality. I think it is up to each person how he or she manages providing others with information regarding medical issues. I, for one, choose to keep my medical issue private. Let it be known, however, my dear reader, that I carry no shame with its diagnosis or its attribution. I mostly find it interpersonally irrelevant.

As you can now understand, I operate from both sides of the mental health treatment paradigm. I am both a mental health provider and a consumer, each of which I have been doing for years. It is from these vantages that I offer you *The Essential Schizophrenia Companion*. I hope you enjoy the read. It is a personal labor of love. Its intent is to lift others up.

CHAPTER 2

JUST THE BASICS

Once the basics of schizophrenia are understood, then we can get to ways of coping. What is schizophrenia? Elementarily devised, most mental health issues can be divided by the parameters of thought versus mood. This delineation is useful when thinking about the generic of schizophrenia.

In a linguistic manner, let us deconstruct the word *schizophrenia*. In the realm of psychological verbiages, the root *schizo* means "thought." The suffix *phrenia* means "compilation." Thus, by sum and translation, we arrive at "a disorder of thought, as compiled"— or in other words, a thought disorder syndrome. Schizophrenia, therefore, is known as a primary thought disorder. When *schizo* is seen in the mental health domain, it can be understood to reflect a thought pathology. As such, schizophrenia belies a primary thought disorder. Its contrast reflects in the major mood disorders, such as bipolar disorder and major depressive disorder. These crudely round out the major mental disorders. The contrasting mood disorders are another topic, my dear reader, so at this point we may further abandon disorders of mood. Ah, the convenient appeals of literary liberties!

Let us delve just a bit further into the conceptualization of schizophrenia. For it is necessary to describe the duck before defeating the duck (you may laugh, but I have known some pesky ducks!). In regard to schizophrenia, it is best to think of it as a syndrome.

This reflects on the suffix portion *phrenia*, which translates to "compilation." So what entails the schizophrenia compilation or, otherwise stated, its syndromic quality?

The schizophrenia syndrome is a constellation. Its composition can be significantly numerable. Its presentation generally voids uniformity. Its application yields by one thousand possibilities and add ten to the top. The number of different types of symptoms ranges from one to twenty, by an approximation. The major symptoms include delusions, auditory hallucinations, and derivative mood disturbance. Many symptoms are subtyped. For example, under delusions, such subtypes include persecutory, erotomanic, grandiose, religious, paranoid, ideas of reference, and somatic. Delusions, as defined, are unsubstantiated or "false beliefs." These can present as a mixed bag. Each person could have any number of these and in various combinations and severities.

Further differentiating delusions, and as elementally discerned, delusions can be evaluated on a broad syntonic-dystonic spectrum. Syntonic delusions are agreeable and favorable to one's intellect or ego. For example, one may believe that he or she has vast wealth that, in actuality, is entirely absent. By contrast, dystonic delusions injure or hurt one's intellect or ego. For example, one may believe he or she is the target of an altogether unsubstantiated evil conspiracy. Each and every delusion can be evaluated on the syntonic-dystonic spectrum. Syntonic delusions can elevate one's sense of self, while dystonic delusions can denigrate oneself. Last, some delusions simply present as characteristically neutral but are nevertheless irrational and unqualified. Such delusions would be midpoint on this spectrum.

Next, as parcel to the greater compilation, we bandy onto auditory hallucinations. These are hallucinations that are, well, auditory. It is hearing words or sentences, or any series of words and sentences, that are not heard by others in the same environment. Auditory hallucinations can vary and characteristically include command and persecutory subtypes. Some hallucinations can also be neutral or otherwise largely effectually benign. Similar to delusions, auditory hallucinations can also be evaluated on the syntonic-dystonic spectrum. Some auditory hallucinations may lift one's disposition while others may trigger turmoil. Auditory hallucinations are difficult for me. They are perhaps the most challenging symptom I endure. I hear them for sure, but they have no true identifiable source. Therefore, I have a hallucinatory status.

The last syndromic component I would like to address is that of mood. Schizophrenia is not a primary mood disorder; rather, it is a primary thought disorder. Nevertheless, schizophrenia comes parcel to its stash of emotions. In my particular instance, paranoia reigns supreme with an associated sense of underlying anxiety. Schizophrenia excites my emotions. It can induce a full range of emotions, from euphoria to blackness and all in between. In a general manner, however, the emotions triggered in me nearly unanimously reside in ample turmoil. When a person believes the world is out to get him or her, happiness becomes a most elusive catch o' the day! But self-pity tends not to dwell in my heart nor reside in my disposition. I have learned to soldier on, as you must, and I again chase my impetus for better times.

Now hold on to your rocket ship, my dear reader, because what follows is the essential literary tour de force, including what I judge to be the most important elements of schizophrenia major. So let us now sink our teeth into the real meat on the bone (or garden burger, if vegetarian)!

CHAPTER 3

ANOSOGNOSIA

Let me not diminish or underestimate the word *anosognosia*. Anosognosia is a paramount consideration in the conceptualization and treatment of schizophrenia. Perhaps more than any other variable, in my opinion, anosognosia resides atop the symptom queue as a primary consideration. What is anosognosia?

Anosognosia is a psychiatric term swiped from the field of neurology and is now aptly applied in psychiatry. As defined, *anosognosia* references one's capacity for cognitive insight. Specifically, anosognosia reflects a "lack of cognitive insight." This concept is a massive consideration to the schizophrenia generic. Allow me to explain why.

In regard to anosognosia and its application to schizophrenia, there are two primary possibilities. Either one has anosognosia or one does not. An individual with schizophrenia who has attributional anosognosia has a cognitive inability to have insight into his or her schizophrenia symptomatology. It follows, therefore, that if anosognosia is absent in one with schizophrenia, the subject then maintains capacity for an intellectual insight into one's associative schizophrenia. As stated, this is overly simplified. Allow me to explain anosognosia further.

In my personal reflections on my schizophrenia, and on schizophrenia in general, I reiterate anosognosia is a most crucial consideration. In my opinion, anosognosia is grossly underestimated and grossly underresearched. From my perspective, anosognosia must be accounted for primarily, foremost, and first. The work of helping someone with schizophrenia without first accounting for and discerning anosognosia will be fruitless and wholly ineffective.

Consider the two primary possibilities: first, those who have schizophrenia but lack anosognosia. In this instance, individuals with schizophrenia have the ability to reflect on their symptoms in a reasonable manner. I am an example of this instance. In other words, I have the cognitive ability to talk about my symptoms at a distance. I am able to process my symptoms intellectually and think about them metacognitively. I can think about the thoughts I am experiencing. I can question and challenge my experienced symptoms. I am able to think or say, for instance, "I just heard a voice that was not there." Then, I can translate that to "I just experienced an auditory hallucination." Next, I can dispel the experience as a constituent symptom of my schizophrenia. Once I identify the thought as an experienced symptom, then I can confidently discard the ensuing experience and provide it no credence. In such an instance, my ability for insight, or my lack of anosognosia, diminishes the symptomatology. I do not have to believe the disturbing symptom and can allow it to benignly pass. Because of insight, which is always in play for me, I can dismiss my symptom rather than believe its content. My intellectual faculties are constantly filtering my experiences for symptoms versus reality. This didactic process never ends, nor can it if I am to conquer schizophrenia.

I use insight across my dimensional schizophrenia syndrome. I use insight in relation to my auditory hallucinations, delusional thought content, and management of related paranoia and derivative anxieties. Managing all these symptoms as they spontaneously occur in my environment becomes the existential challenge. The further challenge is in regard to the psychotic persuasion.

If psychosis were not cognitively persuasive, it would assume no mental occupancy. But psychosis is very persuasive, and rudely so! Its persuasion, however vivid it may seem, falls subject to the faculty of insight. All the schizophrenia nuances, including all the symptoms that present, mutate, and develop in time and over time, must pass through my cognitive filter. My insight is my cognitive filter. And with this filter, I deconstruct my temporal symptoms. I deconstruct, too, the schizophrenia as a whole. I am always earnestly filtering my induced experiences. Only with such a vigilant filter do I survive schizophrenia. Only with a vigilant filter can I present a normalized veneer. But conversely, some with schizophrenia carry the added dimension of anosognosia. By this accord, such an individual has an unlike type of cognitive filter.

For those with anosognosia, symptom processing, otherwise known as reality testing, carries little efficacy. For example, consider an individual with schizophrenia carrying the belief that he is the king of England. When talking with this individual, one may refute the assertion by saying, "You are not the king of England." In reply, he retorts, "I surely am." And although a substantial interpersonal dicker may occur—and even an illusory veneer that surely he does not believe himself to be the king—such a belief can and will persist. One could provide troves of contrary evidence to the assertion, but the cognitive filter, for someone with anosognosia, does not normatively filter reality. And if he concedes that he is not the king of England, the next time you converse, the delusion may have subsided by a degree, only to be replaced by the belief that he is the prince of Wales. Then, the process will recycle. For those with anosognosia, the metacognitive (the ability to think about one's thoughts) filter does not properly filter reality. Delusions accumulate, and a permanent sort of altered reality capably ensues. And from the external observing lens, such an individual will appear to be entirely and persistently psychotic, substantially out of touch with reality.

Last, in regard to anosognosia, is this primary and eminent consideration. When interacting with someone with schizophrenia with anosognosia, a concession must occur. If one does not have the capacity for insight due to anosognosia, psychosis is going to stubbornly persist. Lacking such insight, there just is no manner to bring someone back to the viable and customary type of shared reality. With anosognosia, psychosis will persistently prevail with little recourse for a full transformation back to our shared reality. This is not to say that those with schizophrenia with anosognosia do not have moments of lucidity. They do. Further, despite a prevailing psychosis, one certainly can present with a sort of charm and even wisdom. However, a gainful reconciliation to the normative reality will be untenable.

When trying to help someone with schizophrenia, anosognosia must be primarily discerned. Trying to counterreason with someone with anosognosia is like a dog chasing its tail. Bringing said individual back to the common reality just isn't gonna happen, at least not entirely. And if one delusion indeed is negated, another will likely replace it. There's simply no manner of inducing the normative reality construct. The cognitive filter does not normatively filter, and a persistent psychosis prevails. When this is the case, it is best to interact with such an individual not with repeated challenges but with an artful acquiescence. Interacting with such an individual can be elegant. Having a relationship with such an individual can be endearing and provocative. The filter does not filter, but the beloved one immersed in the psychotic throes remains. To best relate to such an individual, one must learn to be a psychosis whisperer. Love, to and fro, still avails. It is just a different-looking type of relationship. Rationality must take a knee, in part, and creativity in relating must muscle up. Beyond any hesitation or doubt, it can yet be a wonderful type of loving relationship. So, anosognosia or not, there's no need to ever abandon hope!

The question becomes, "Is anosognosia an all-or-nothing capacity?" In other words, Can one develop capacity for insight, or is it innate? There are different theories as to the answer. Some contend that insight can develop and be taught. Others think it is innate and a zero-sum game. The general research on the topic has no clear-cut answer, and so we dwell amid speculation. If there's one area lacking in the schizophrenia research, this is it! Anosognosia is an enormous construct in relation to all aspects of the schizophrenia syndrome. When the topic of schizophrenia is brought up, the first consideration as to its potential remedies must be the presence, or lack thereof, of anosognosia. With anosognosia primarily discerned in each, then the treatment protocols follow. Further, the solution to relating with someone will follow by its dictate.

When the word *schizophrenia* is mentioned, your next thought should be, "Anosognosia or not?" Once this is clearly discerned, then all pertinent protocols follow. "Schizophrenia? Hmm. Anosognosia or not?" With this question and answer, unnecessary burdens are lifted from the lives of all involved. Trust me on this one!

Ultimately, you may want to know if anosognosia is developmental, teachable, or innate. In my opinion, not subject to any research, I find it innate rather than developmental. If one has capacity for insight, full, gainful recovery is possible. If one is positive for anosognosia, full recovery is improbable, if not impossible. Relating to this intrinsic variable in those with schizophrenia is a paramount consideration. Please keep this prevalent in your thoughts on schizophrenia when the topic is broached. You'll be glad you did!

Last, remember even those with anosognosia can maintain lasting and loving relationships. Anosognosia is no value judgment. It is simply a schizophrenia symptom. Those with schizophrenia with anosognosia are no different than you or me. Such individuals are just tapped into another type of reality. I advise you to enjoy this otherworldliness. I can assure you that you will find it most fascinating and wholly endearing!

CHAPTER 4

PARADOX

Once anosognosia is capably discerned, the variable of insight follows. Insight into schizophrenia can constantly evolve. When a person does not have anosognosia and adheres to a prescribed medication regimen, insight can mightily pacify schizophrenia. Insight is one's generalized understanding of one's schizophrenia. It can also be specific to the parts of schizophrenia. Insight is one's understanding of the symptoms followed by one's learned manners for coping. It involves many variables and depends on multiple cognitive faculties and perspectives. For now, my dear reader, in regard to a singular ingredient of insight, let us delve into paradox.

I vigorously attest that schizophrenia is an inherently paradoxical syndrome. If one is going to conquer schizophrenia, an understanding of the disorder as paradoxical is imperative. Unless one's medication regimen entirely obliterates all schizophrenia symptoms, insight must be used to promote recovery. And without understanding schizophrenia as paradoxical, full, gainful recovery will be elusive. Therefore, the question becomes, How is schizophrenia a paradoxical syndrome?

To best explain its paradoxical nature, allow me to first describe its experience. As I go about my day, I will hear things others do not. I certainly hear voices from the environment, but others in the same environment do not. Let us add a delusional belief to the scenario. Because of hearing repeated persecutory voices, I develop a sort of persecutory delusion. A delusion is nothing more than a false belief, lacking in shared evidence. To top this psychotic sundae, my dear reader, let us add a shaky anxiety with related paranoia. Let us now assume that I am at a holiday picnic. I am experiencing auditory hallucinations, accompanied by a related delusion and wrapped in a schizophrenia bow by an associated paranoia and anxiety. Now, how does this relate to paradox?

First, I must assert that, while all these symptoms of mine are swirling about, they seem entirely truthful. In such situations things get awfully challenging, including acting the normative and reasonable part. Sometimes it is difficult to talk with someone about the weather, for example, while in your own mind you think he or she may want you to go to hell, both literally and figuratively. But by manner of trial and error, and over the course of two-plus decades, I have learned that a type of behavioral rationality is always best. So, again, how is such an experience paradoxical?

The answer to this question begins with my use of insight. Remember insight allows me to cope with schizophrenia. So here I am, at a picnic, in a near-delusional terror. To me, the timbre of the frolicking picnic is anything but. Wherever I set my gaze, things feel out of control and significantly persecutory. But over the many years, I have learned not to be so hasty in my judgment and not to give up. And remember, my dear reader, as trite as it may sound, "never give up" is a most prudent course of action. So rather than further submerging in my cognitive terror, I have learned some tricks to tread in such tumultuous waters. I have learned the faculty of insight. And an essential ingredient to the whole of an able cognitive insight is the understanding of the schizophrenia generic as an inherently paradoxical rendering and malaise.

The paradox belies as such. I hear voices. I believe certain insanities. I derivatively emote, in toxicity. But here is the pardon: I have learned that my cognitive representations are false. My perceptions are false. My experience rests on a bedrock of untruth. It has taken me many years of trial and error to conclude that my schizophrenia induced angst is primarily intrapsychic and not interpsychic. My turmoil resides as a product of my own brain and mind. Such a conclusion I have tested for decades now. Sometimes my experiences are awful and even traumatic. But my suffering and trauma, I have discovered, are internally derivative and not externally derivative. They come from within and are not relational.

Given this pretext, therefore, here is the operative paradox. Because my reality-testing faculties are bruised, my internal self-talk must reflect the following sentiments: "That which I see, I do not; that which I hear, I do not; that which I believe, I do not; that which I feel lacks the evidence." This is the paradox of schizophrenia. Its malaise is rendered via the avenue of the presumptive reality. Its symptoms twist and distort my reality construct. But at the same time, schizophrenia is not invulnerable. Its gaping weakness is its paradoxical nature and characteristics. If schizophrenia did not have this innate vulnerability, recovery would be neglectful. Any alternatives to its rendering would be forgone. But schizophrenia does have a shake to its knees. Its rendering is paradoxical. Its approach is a known quality. Its activity is a known sort. Its application invades and intrudes by paradox. Because human beings are inherently metacognitive, schizophrenia lacks a coherent unity. Psychosis and schizophrenia can deconstruct under the power of metacognitive reflection, and this ably deflects the schizophrenia rendering and malaise. But this can only be done by recognition of schizophrenia as inherently paradoxical. And once you become comfortable with routine cognitive paradox, miracles happen, and yet twice again!

CHAPTER 5

BEHAVIORAL RATIONALITY

Behavioral rationality is a personally coined phrase of mine. It means that, amid all mental circumstances, cognitive knots, and a prevailing psychosis, I nevertheless practice a sort of manneristic reasonableness.

The approach to behavioral rationality is this: Let us assume I am psychotic. And let's pretend, again, that I am at a jovial holiday picnic. In this hypothetical sketch, let us attribute the following to my active mental status. For our purposes, let us assume delusions, auditory hallucinations, and paranoia are my current cognitive-affective cohorts. Due to my insight, I am self-talking to the hilt to cognitively mitigate this psychotic bite. But beyond such a cognitive approach, I too have learned essential *behaviors*. Behavioral rationality resides within the behavioral coping specs, rather than the cognitive realm. Together with my cognitive manipulations of self-talk, I have pieced together a sort of behavioral skill set. This I label *behavioral rationality*.

So I reside in a psychotic state of mind. How do I practice behavioral rationality? I must confess, my dear reader, I have conditioned my behavior more than my thoughts. I have found that eliminating cognitive pathology is a most difficult and laborious task. Thoughts can be spurious, and this is universal. Thoughts can blip on the radar screen or fire like an unstable electron. I'm not saying that control in a cognitive sense is not possible. It is, at least to a certain degree. But in terms of behavior, I've discovered a level of control beyond the mere cognitive. Let me explain what I mean.

Thoughts are constituents of the cognitive realm. Behaviors are constituents of the behavioral realm. The two are distinct although influential of each other. Behaviors include speech characteristics, or the things one says, as well as one's approach to interpersonal relations. One can be said to be easygoing, kind, or affectionate. One could be rude, inappropriate, or vulgar. One could be gentle, humble, or caring.

Behaviors also include body language. Such language is well known to us, and it usually is quite easily appraised. For example, one's body language can be relaxed, nervous, or fearful. Oftentimes, it is a natural and innate type of personality disposition. At other times, however, it may be most helpful to be behaviorally deliberate or directive. This is where behavioral rationality emerges.

Behavioral rationality means being behaviorally appropriate to the given social context. It means to steadfastly remain in the proper environmental context without any overt or ridiculous unreasonableness. It directs the avoidance of speaking out of proper context. Schizophrenia is often highly correlated with contextually poor language verbalizations. Those with schizophrenia often speak out of the rational interpersonal context, in statements derivative of delusions.

All in all, behavioral rationality means monitoring my environment for the most appropriate and reasonable behaviors. If someone says, "Hi, Robert! How are you today?" I will gleefully reply (because I am a wholly gleeful type of person, my dear reader, lest we forget our need for levity), "I am well, and you?" I do not say that the people lurking in the background are apparently conspiring against me. I do not declare that the voices I hear are telling me that I am in a version of hell. I keep the cognitive purely cognitive. My cognitive and behavioral activities remain entirely distinct. So when my cognitive pathology fires, I behave in rational accord. And with some practice, this becomes easier over time. I am now an all-star (a baseball reference—I happen to be a Red Sox fan) at controlling my behavior according to context. Once my behavior is well under wraps, persisting in my environment of a normalized accord avails. And with this a gainful sort of life sustenance ensues. Controlling my behavior is a personal dictate of mine. I demand it of myself. It is the only way to remain fully participatory in all aspects of life.

Behavioral rationality, for me, is now habitual. I use it all the time—every day and every hour. It is one of my tricks of the general schizophrenia trade (I happen to be in the schizophrenia union, local 107). I demand of myself a vigilant behavioral rationality despite the presenting symptomatic cognitive turmoil. And for me, this has been an absolute game changer!

CHAPTER 6

PROTECTIVE FACTORS

Protective factors are essential in coping with schizophrenia. Protective factors are items of a personal choosing that aid (but do not abet, lest we forget our good humor) in sustained recovery. Without good use of protective factors, schizophrenia roars. But I have tamed the lion some, and it abhors such protections.

A primary protective factor in my life is my choosing of psychiatric medicine. I've taken the same antipsychotic medication for over twenty-five years. Oftentimes the topic of antipsychotics (or even psychiatric meds generally) becomes a bone of philosophical contention. Of course, most psychiatrists are advocates of their use. Such medications are in the absolute wheelhouse (another baseball reference) for most psychiatrists!

On the other hand, a counterculture exists of folks who look most critically upon the use of psychiatric meds. By and by, whether pro or con, this medicinal push-pull has existed to and fro since the advent of psychiatry, and I do not think it will resolve in my lifetime. For me, my medication works. I take it, and it helps tremendously. I carry no qualms as to its ingestion. But as far as my recommendations to others in regard to either taking psychiatric meds or not, I believe it best left to the sound judgment of each.

By a historical context, I offer a bit more about my medication. In my very early psychiatric history, in my twenties, I tried haloperidol and then olanzapine. Neither were very effective for me other than inducing ample lethargy accompanied by a significant type of mental fog. After failing on both of these med trials, I was at once started on clozapine. The day I started taking clozapine, I was already in an inpatient psychiatric unit. I was floridly psychotic. Its use was discussed with my family, and I agreed to its trial. Some three days after the initial dosages, I mostly returned to my rational faculties. The turnaround with its application was remarkable. From my own psychological perspective, I felt like myself once again. My delusions and auditory hallucinations substantially subsided. I could think and move again. I felt drastically improved.

Because the topic of medication is so darn important to the greater schizophrenia equation, I want to amplify a bit more. I have been taking two hundred milligrams of clozapine each night for twenty-five years without increase or decrease. Each and every month, I am required to get a routine ANC bloodwork panel completed before my medicine can be dispensed by the pharmacy. In the bloodwork, the measure of pertinence is my immunity levels. Clozapine has the rare side effect of agranulocytosis, a term that indicates a depleted white blood cell count or a decrease in my immune system's ability to fight off infections. So each month, my immune system gets a look under the hood. By an estimate, in twenty-five years taking clozapine, I've had five to eight occasions of reduced immunity. And each instance when the bloodwork was repeated, as is required, my immunity was found to again be within normal limits. So it is clozapine each night until my comfy grave beckons. For me, it works. I have no complaints. It is a primary protective factor, and I have no quibble (or nibble, lest we forget, my dear reader, our capacity for levity).

In terms of protective factors, allow me to add a few more. For me, talking to a therapist or counselor helps. I used to see a therapist more regularly than I do now, but because I am now a schizophrenia all-pro (a football reference), I see my therapist about once every six weeks or thereabouts. When I go, I set the agenda for what I want to speak about. During the two to three days prior to going, I usually generate a written list of my agenda items. Then, during my sessions, I will test the reality of some of my disturbing experiences with my therapist. Almost all my described psychotic experiences lack sufficient evidence according to my beliefs. But admittedly, like an LP playing over and over again, I never tire of the feedback that my perceptions lack the needed evidence to sustain my cognitive delusion. It's always reassuring to hear from my therapist that my perceptions were significantly distorted. I smile and laugh at my own insanities. Then, I talk about other items of my choosing.

Let us not get long in the tooth regarding protective factors (I've always wanted to use that expression, and now I have!). So more succinctly, here are a few other pertinent protective factors. I do not drink or take drugs. I exercise regularly, including lifting weights and running. I sleep well and maintain a proper sleep schedule. Family relationships soothe my sometimes weary soul. Knowing that others support me assuages my psychotic wounds. I try not to engage in self-pity. Schizophrenia happens to be my specified lot, and I try not to feel sorry for myself. I do not ask, "Why me?" (I accepted my schizophrenia long ago.) I enjoy playing sports, especially with my niece and nephews, and I love to watch sports on TV. I am a fantasy football enthusiast (and one-time champ). I happen to enjoy being alone and spend a lot of time as such. I prefer being solitary for the most part. I'll take a pass on the party, picnic, or night on the town. I find being alone peaceful.

My last protective factor is my faith in God. Without God, I would've been basted, fried, cooked, sizzled, and sliced and diced a long, long time ago. In my life, God indeed is an "amazing grace," and He indeed "saved a wretch like me." 'Nuff said on that, right?

CHAPTER 7

PHILOSOPHY OF MIND

Good books are not good books without a little philosophy. Don't you agree, my dear reader? I think much life wisdom is derivative of philosophy. In fact, most pithy idioms of eternal wisdom usually sound philosophical. Some say philosophy has little pragmatism. It certainly cannot start a motor or cause a boat to float, but it can assist when the motor is broken and the boat sinks. So how does philosophy pertain to schizophrenia?

Within the greater realm of the philosophy generic dwells a subsidiary canon known as the philosophy of mind, the study of the immaterial within each of us— the mind. The word *mind*, representing the immaterial within, can easily adapt to different verbiages, so whatever your particular preference is can apply. For instance, rather than *mind*, some may call it spirit, soul, or waking consciousness. All these terms point to the immaterial in all of us. The mind is the very item that escapes the otherwise biologic known as human.

Schizophrenia is a pathology that is significantly mind-based in its placement. Yes, schizophrenia dwells within the parameters of its biological, neurological, or genetic correlates. But additionally and certainly, schizophrenia rents occupancy in the human immeasurable—that is, in the immaterial mind. In the subsidiary philosophical canon known as philosophy of mind follows a primary tenet, although it is as yet hypothetical. This tenet is the assumption that each member of humankind has a distinct entity within that is separate from all the rest. In other words, each person has his or her own mind that is separate from everyone else's. This tenet, and its notion, is nearly universally accepted as a basic human constituent. Largely, people see themselves as separate entities from their neighbors, both by a biological delineation and by a mind delineation. And when you examine humanity's existence through a sociological lens, this very presumption of differentiated minds powers the nature of our interactions and our lives. It is a presumption, I think, that is often taken for granted. We bandy about believing we are differentiated and inherently interactional.

Schizophrenia, however, routinely confronts this global assumption. Those with schizophrenia, myself included, regularly have experiences external of this primary tenet. Each and every day, I wonder if my mind is indeed differentiated from the rest. I tell you, and frankly so, that many of my symptoms are products of my mind's struggle with its own differentiation. Philosophy of mind ordains that you have your private mind and I have my private mind. But because of my schizophrenia, such a basic sense of differentiation often eludes me. Minds feel connected. And in such a perception of connectedness can ensue the symptoms of delusions, auditory hallucinations, and feelings of paranoia. If I could habitually feel a certain type of differentiated mind, I think some of my symptoms would decrease. The "fact" that each and every person has a differentiated mind from the rest is a difficult proposition for me to fully appreciate. Sometimes my mind does feel separate from others but not all the time. So the greater point is this: You cannot assume that people with schizophrenia experience their minds like you do yours. Many people with schizophrenia, if you listen to their stated "delusions," will reflect a reality that challenges the very presumption of differentiated minds.

Last, when trying to help people with schizophrenia reduce their symptoms, this very framework regarding differentiation can be brought up and discussed. You may be surprised at your findings! I have many difficult experiences, persecutory ones included, that derive from this very essence. My mind does not always feel differentiated, but I have come to recognize this conundrum. When I think to myself, after a psychotic experience, that all the people I interacted with indeed had separate and private minds of their own, as do I, reality sheds its wholesome light again. But I must also attest that the feelings of connectedness garnered by schizophrenia ever so rarely produce a slight tinge of sublimity. By and by, however, please be aware of the pertinent variable known as the philosophy of mind when talking to or treating someone with schizophrenia. It just may be significantly palliative!

CHAPTER 8

RESEARCH

I want to briefly talk about the modern research on schizophrenia. Around the globe and across the United States, schizophrenia is being researched. I want to address research because I think it is important both as a source of hope and inspiration as well as a notice of its impressive and developing science. Many an expenditure is levied on schizophrenia. The scopes of these studies are variable.

Again, please do not misconstrue me as scientific. *The Essential Schizophrenia Companion* is a work of the humanities and not science. Nevertheless, from my own personal bank of learning about the research on schizophrenia, allow me these few items.

Schizophrenia is sliced, diced, and parsed from all imaginable angles. Its research involves the topics of etiology, medicinals, and treatment protocols. Its research is vast, and it is a lengthy proposal if one seeks its full parameters. But with what follows, you will know the most fundamental propositions. I wholly assure you!

As far as its possible etiology, for one, schizophrenia is researched via brain activity. In our modernity, brain imaging is now prolific and then some. Science can now declare many derivatives from the study of the brain. For our purposes, my dear reader, let us simply know that the human brain, according to its every existing nook, is being robustly studied for neurological illuminations, including on schizophrenia.

Modern science is now too immersed in genetic research. The genetic field is relatively new but is now exploding. Modern science endeavors to understand the entire mapping of the human genome. Scientists from around the world are collaborating on specified genome projects, with some being conducted on the psychiatric morbidities, including schizophrenia. Genetic research is emerging as a new front-runner in understanding the etiology of schizophrenia. Of course, once etiology can be fully discerned, then its recourse would follow.

Further schizophrenia research involves the pharmaceuticals, or medicinals. Medicinals are always being studied, created, and refined. Novel mechanisms routinely reside on the horizon. Certain mechanisms of action are heavily analyzed. Medicinal interrogations are heavily parcel to the greater body of schizophrenia research.

Interventions, from a psychosocial perspective, are highly relevant to the schizophrenia canon. The question in this realm becomes, How can a person with schizophrenia be best helped from the interpersonal and social domains? Practitioners in this realm focus on what works best from a psychological and social approach, and their findings are typically executed by the mental health talk-therapy experts and practitioners. These include psychiatrists, psychologists, and social workers, among the greater group. Such therapy ideally centers on what type of intervention works best for a specific person. Approaches include cognitive-behavioral therapy (CBT), reality testing, cognitive remediation, and psychoanalysis. These interpersonal approaches are significantly researched, and the best approaches (known clinically as best practices) have been developed and refined. Similar to all canons, all such interventions must be continually refined and updated. And of course, all such canons also aspire to innovation and ultimately to finding the curative.

So, my dear reader, while you and I rest our weary heads atop our fluffy pillows, scientists around the world are investigating schizophrenia from all angles and potentials. Given this, we should all sleep well at night knowing that the proper work in the schizophrenia sciences is being conducted, and vigorously so. I offer this chapter as a pragmatic knowledge base. I also offer it by course of a most ample hope! Hope, my dear reader, is the ultimate body electric!

CHAPTER 9

PUTTING IT ALL TOGETHER

Schizophrenia is a complex puzzle for each to manage. It affects both the individual and the related family. In coping with the schizophrenia syndrome, I have personally reconciled with its imposition. It surely is no fun to endure it, but why quibble on the details? In life, no one is exempt from hassle and challenge. It seems to me, by manner of a type of shared humanity, that we all are placed on this beautiful globe for reasons of personal transcendence. Can we overcome our challenges? Do our personal challenges edify us or cause us to whither? Can we surmount rather than succumb? Schizophrenia is a difficult illness, but it can also be conceived as parcel to the much greater collectives of human disease, malaise, and affliction. And so, if you or your family are affected by schizophrenia, take heart. Like all matters, by course of an able psychological adjustment, sustenance avails. Hope avails. Love yet avails.

The constituents to the schizophrenia puzzle comprise many interlocking availabilities. It is the combination of these pieces, and how they fit together, that ultimately unifies one's being and one's worldly experience. Schizophrenia is not a coda. It is a journey like any other. If not outright defeated, schizophrenia can be managed. An ample acclimation can occur both individually and as nested in the greater family system.

A man I admire is a veteran of the Vietnam War and resides at a nursing home. In my role as a talk therapist, he is a client of mine. But I rather think it is me who is the receiver of wisdom and insight. For you see, this man is bedridden. His legs are deformed and unusable. Due to a massive stroke, he is paralyzed on his left side, and due to dysphagia (inadequate swallowing muscles), he is on a permanent feeding tube. He cannot consume any food or drink by mouth. Further, due to his stroke, he cannot articulate in fluid language. He can make expressive sounds but no words. Although he cannot speak, he is cognitively lucid. His memory is capable, and he is not confused. When we interact, we use hand gestures and writing to communicate with each other. We have also developed some shared communication nuances. Sometimes he can finish my thoughts, and sometimes I can finish his gesticulations.

I mention this great man because, each and every time I see him and ask him how he is, in the general, he quickly responds with an affirmative thumbs-up. I have known this man for over two years, and he has never lodged a complaint (other than needing to be readjusted in his bed). I admire this man. He puts things into proper perspective. He never pities himself, and he never complains. He has accepted his malaise and has transcended. Every time I see him, I relay my esteem for his attitude. He teaches me that there's no reason for ample self-pity. I thank him for teaching me the value of acceptance followed by transcendence.

Please do not carry the burden of schizophrenia on your shoulders as an insurmountable levy. It is not. If relegation does not work, coping avails. It is a challenge, but we all must at one time answer the bell. The bell rings for thee! This idiom, I find, reflects a unanimous and universal experience. At one time or another, we all must answer the personal bell chime. We all must endure our human stature, schizophrenia or otherwise.

I have now compiled the most pertinent information I can fathom to assist and manage the schizophrenia syndrome. I have tried to provide some of the tools, ideas, and coping means that I have used to gainfully overcome schizophrenia. Education on the syndrome is so essential. My hope is that I provided a few nuggets of applicable use.

I have outlined the basics I think you need to know to assist you and your family in overcoming schizophrenia. Putting all the pertinent pieces together is the challenge. Yes, it is challenging, but it is also very possible. Remember, the worst-case scenario resides in a capable adjustment both for the individual and the related family system. Panacea may evade, but ample social adjustment is always entirely possible. Take heart!

Sometimes I laugh rather than cry. Humor is essential in my life, especially in my ability to deal with psychosis. For me, laughter is a significant protective factor. I have learned to find humor in my psychosis, albeit retrospectively. When amid psychosis, it is disturbing. After its episodic experience passes and fades, it's peculiarities and absurdities often trigger in me a sort of welcome humor and chuckle. In other words, psychosis can be so bizarre that it ultimately lends to a type of personally recognized humor. It's okay to laugh at psychosis. Sometimes, retrospectively, it is downright amusing, especially according to its bizarre insanities. "Laugh, clown, laugh" provides me sufficient coping. I have said more than once that if you cannot laugh at your troubles by some angle or accord, you will be cooked and consumed. Laughter is a melody to the soul!

The pieces to my schizophrenia puzzle may not entirely match yours. This is why the relegation of schizophrenia is best suited as a collegial and open-ended enterprise. We can learn a lot from one another. But for now, my dear reader, we depart from our shared company. So, while you tame your lion, I will try and do the same. And in our mutual transcendence, at once, we shall together laugh again and share in our regales. But for now, I wish you fond travels, my beloved.

GLOSSARY

Common and not-so-common symptoms known in schizophrenia for your easy reference, my dear reader.

amotivation: A psychiatric symptom characterized by a lack of goal-directed behavior.

anosognosia: A clinical term indicating a lack of prevailing insight into one's mental illness, usually pertaining to schizophrenia.

auditory hallucination: A psychiatric symptom indicating the presence of voices heard singularly by an individual that are absent to others; such hallucinations often cause emotional distress.

catatonic behavior: Behavior characterized by a hyperbolic lack of physical movement.

command auditory hallucination: A psychiatric symptom indicating a specified type of auditory hallucination with characteristic impelled directives.

delusion: A psychiatric symptom indicating a false belief. Delusions can be clinically differentiated according to thematic type. A delusion entails thought content that is personally believed but is highly irrational (and likely impossible) to rational people.

dysphoric: A psychiatric term indicating a significant emotional disturbance with a characteristic severe depression.

dystonic delusion: A psychiatric term referencing the acute cognitive status of a prevailing false and disagreeable belief, according to one's intellect or ego. It typically infers an emotionally disturbed status.

erotomanic delusion: A specified type of delusion or false belief involving a believed romantic-type relationship. The other is often conceived as a celebrity or other famous person.

flat affect: A psychiatric presentation or appearance inferring a persistently depressed or quasi-depressed emotional climate; highly correlated with schizophrenia and classified as a negative symptom.

ideas of reference: A specified type of delusion that involves unrelated and innocuous events that come with perceptions of association and pertinence and are psychologically disturbing.

incongruent affect: A psychiatric symptom indicating an irrational correlation, or a mismatch, between one's mood and one's thought or speech. It is indicative of one's cognitive status and found primarily in those with thought disorders.

mind reading: A psychiatric symptom characterized by the delusional belief that one can directly communicate with others by means of mind-to-mind exchanges (without need for overt speech); such exchanges are believed possible irrespective of spatial proximity.

negative symptoms: A psychiatric term indicating a group of symptoms often found in a *schizo* disorder (or thought disorder).

poverty of speech: A psychiatric symptom indicating the lack of a normalized quantity of speech over time (i.e., markedly minimal verbalizations).

poverty of thought: A psychiatric symptom indicating the lack of a normalized quantity of thought over time (i.e., few thoughts over time).

religious ideation: A psychiatric symptom indicating the presence of ideas or notions with typical religious or spiritual themes and overtones.

self-dialoguing: A psychiatric symptom indicating the behavioral phenomenon of talking aloud to oneself, usually in response to auditory hallucinations or delusions.

syntonic delusion: A psychiatric term referencing the acute cognitive status of a prevailing agreeable but false belief, according to one's own intellect or ego.

thought blocking: A psychiatric symptom indicating the lack of a normalized succession to one's thoughts.

thought broadcasting: A psychiatric symptom characterized by the delusional belief that one's thoughts are being projected into the environment and heard verbatim by others.

thought disorder: A generalized psychiatric categorization and moniker indicating a specified set of diagnostics (i.e., schizophrenia and its related symptoms).

www.ingramcontent.com/pod-product-compliance
Lightning Source LLC
Chambersburg PA
CBHW051420250726
48655CB00003B/1150